# MAO ZEDONG
## THE FOUNDING FATHER OF CHINA

Biography of Famous People

Children's Biography Books

Mao Zedong, who is also known as Mao Tse-tung, was the leader of China's Communist Party. He is mostly remembered as the Founding Father of the People's Republic of China. In this book, you will be learning about his life and his accomplishments.

# BIOGRAPHY

Mao Zedong was the founder of the People's Republic of China and was its main leader from its establishment in 1949 until 1976, when he died. He was also the leader of China's communist revolution and fought during the Chinese Civil War against the Nationalist Party. Mao's philosophies and ideas about communism and Marxism became known as Maoism.

MAO ZEDONG MONUMENT

SHAOSHAN

# WHERE WAS HE RAISED?

Mao was born in Shaoshan, Hunan Province, China on December 26, 1893. His father was Mao Yichang, a peasant farmer, and his mother was Wen Qimei. He had three siblings; two brothers and a sister. He went to a local school until the age of 13 when he started working on his family's farm full time.

He joined the Revolution Army in 1911, fighting against the Qing Dynasty. He then went back to school and he took a job working as a librarian.

THE IMPERIAL PALACE OF THE QING DYNASTY

STATUE OF SUN YAT-SEN

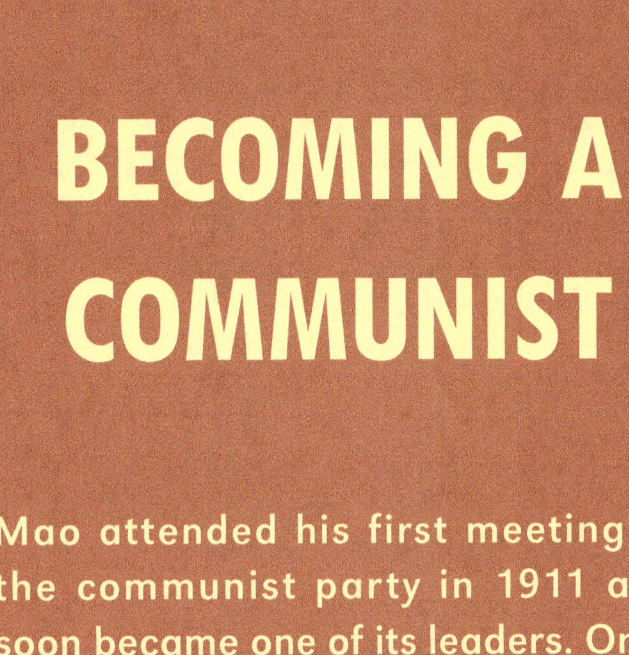

# BECOMING A COMMUNIST

Mao attended his first meeting of the communist party in 1911 and soon became one of its leaders. Once the communists had allied with the Kuomintang, he went to Hunan to work for Sun Yat-sen.

Since he was raised as a peasant, he strongly
believed in the ideas of communism. Mao learned
about Marxism and believed communism to be the
best way to get the peasants to follow him and
overthrow the government.

MAO ZEDONG

CHINESE NATIONALIST SOLDIERS

# CHINESE CIVIL WAR

In 1925, following the death of President Sun Yat-sen, Chiang Kai-shek took the government over as well as the Nationalist Party (also known as the Kuomintang). Chiang decided that he did not want the communists to be a part of his government anymore and broke his communist alliance and starting imprisoning and killing the communist leaders. This was the beginning of the Chinese Civil War between the communists and the Nationalist Party.

Following many years of battle, the Nationalist Party made the decision to once and for all destroy the communists. Kai-shek, along with a million soldiers, attacked the communist's main camp. Zedong persuaded the leaders to retreat.

MAO ZEDONG

THE LONG MARCH
The communist retreat from the Kuomintang army is now known as the Long March. During the span of a year, Zedong led the communists more than 7,000 miles across the southern part of China and then to the Shaanxi province, located in the northern part of China.

Even though 8,000 soldiers survived the march, most of them died, and the remaining 8,000 soldiers became loyal to Zedong. He was now leader of the communist party (also referred to as the CPC).

The War had subsided once Japan invaded China during WWII, but quickly started up again following the war and with Mao in charge, the communists were now stronger. They were soon able to rout the Kuomintang and Chiang Kai-shek fled to Taiwan.

WORLD WAR II

MAO ZEDONG

# FOUNDING THE PEOPLE'S REPUBLIC OF CHINA

Mao founded the People's Republic of China in 1949. He was now the Chairman of the Communist Party as well as the leader of China. Known to be a fierce leader, he maintained his power by killing anyone that disagreed with his beliefs. In addition, he sent millions of people to labor camps that he had set up, where many died.

# THE GREAT LEAP FORWARD

Mao announced in 1985 that he had a plan for industrializing China and named it the Great Leap Forward. His plan backfired and the country soon went on to experience horrible famine. Approximately 40 million people died from starvation.

POPE URBAN II PREACHING THE FIRST CRUSADE

This terrible failure caused him to lose his power for a while. He remained part of the government, however, he did not have absolute power.

# THE CULTURAL REVOLUTION

Mao would make his comeback in 1966 during the Cultural Revolution. Several young peasants followed Mao and they formed what became known as the Red Guard, and these soldiers assisted him in taking over. They closed the schools and anyone in disagreement with him either was murdered or sent off to farms for re-education using hard labor.

换新天
POSTER OF THE CULTURAL REVOLUTION OF CHINA

Quotations
of chairman
Mao Zedong

Part of his comeback was fueled by the "Little Red Book", which was a red book of his sayings that was available to everyone.

In 1972, Mao met with President Nixon in an effort to show his openness to the west. Since Mao's health was declining, Nixon met mostly with Zhou Enlai, who was second in command to Mao. This meeting became an important part of the Cold War since China had begun moving closer to the United States, and apart from the Soviet Union.

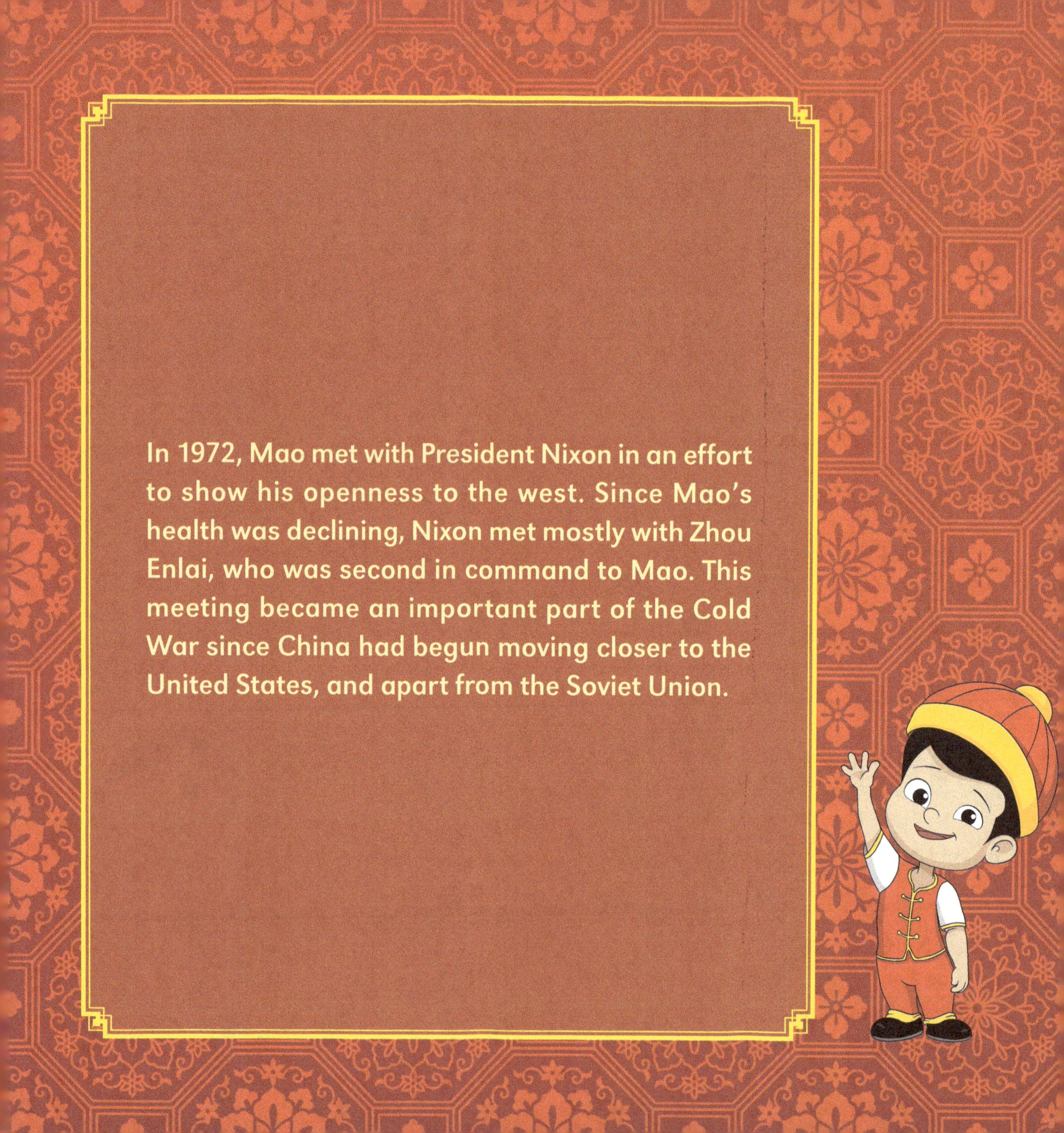

ZHOU ENLAI

MAO ZEDONG YOUTH ART SCULPTURE

Mao is usually credited with uniting China as a country as well as making it a major power during the 20th century. He did this, however, with the loss of millions of lives.

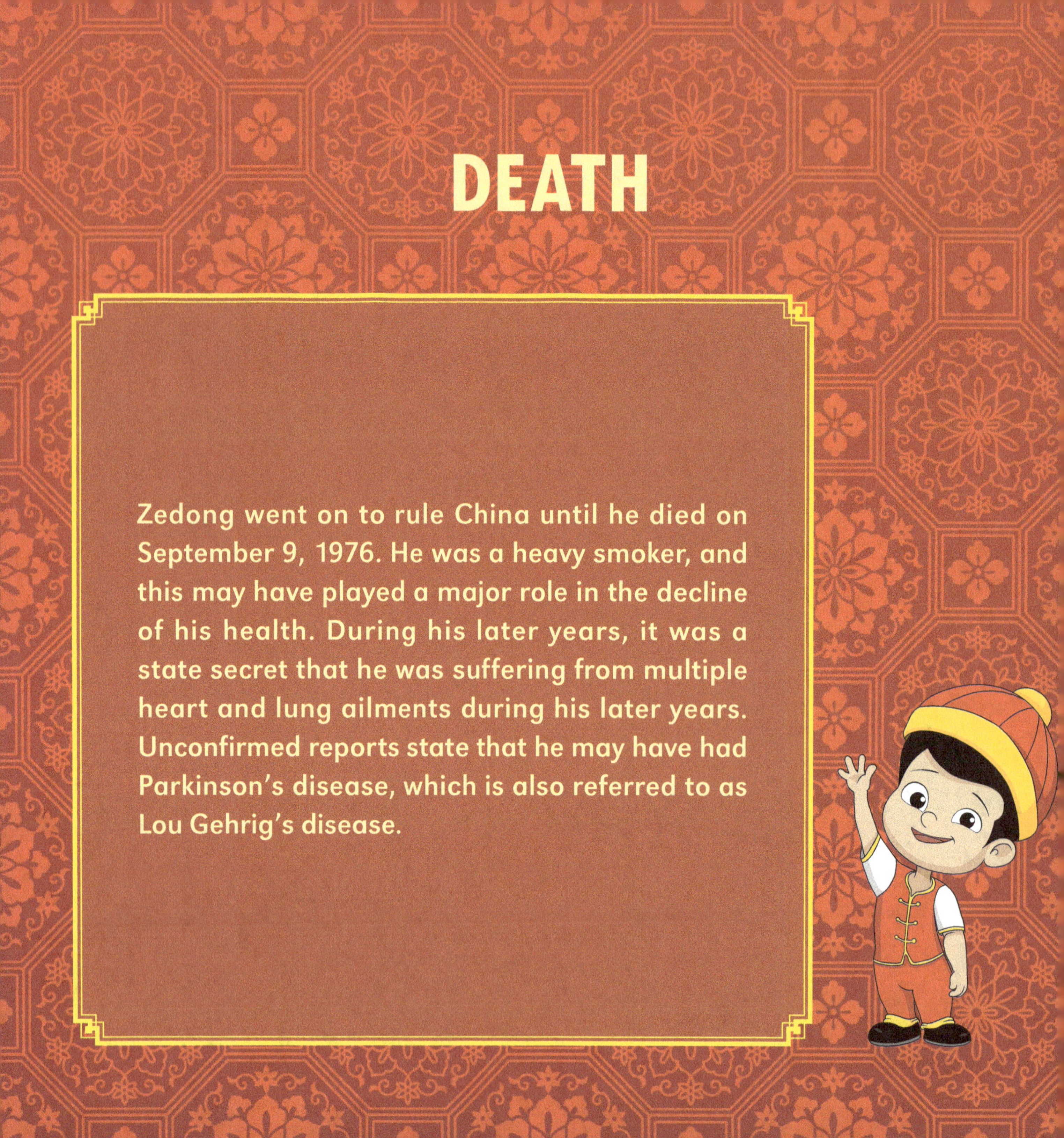

# DEATH

Zedong went on to rule China until he died on September 9, 1976. He was a heavy smoker, and this may have played a major role in the decline of his health. During his later years, it was a state secret that he was suffering from multiple heart and lung ailments during his later years. Unconfirmed reports state that he may have had Parkinson's disease, which is also referred to as Lou Gehrig's disease.

# THE MAUSOLEUM OF CHAIRMAN MAO ZEDONG

COMMUNIST NEW FOURTH ARMY

# THE CHINESE CIVIL WAR

The lengthy Chinese Civil War occurred between 1927 and 1950. It was interrupted in 1936 when China was invaded by Japan, as well as during World War II. It was fought amongst China's nationalist government, also referred to as the Kuomintang, and the Communist Party of China.

# LEADERS

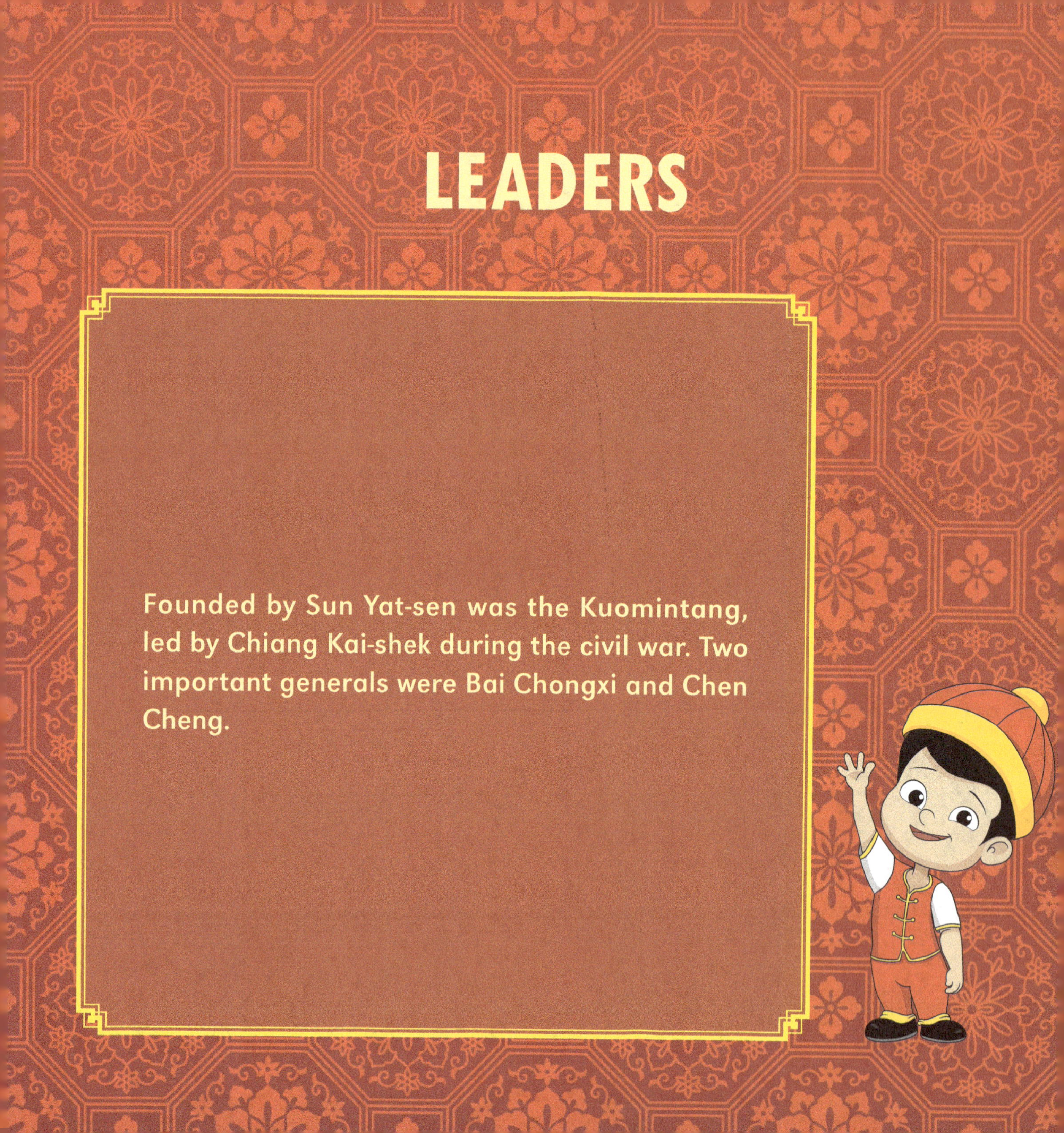

Founded by Sun Yat-sen was the Kuomintang, led by Chiang Kai-shek during the civil war. Two important generals were Bai Chongxi and Chen Cheng.

SUN YAT-SEN SCULPTURE

COMMUNIST STATUE MONUMENTS OF CHINA

Led by Mao Zedong was the Communist Party of China, also known as the CPC. The second in command was Zhou Enlai and two generals Zhu De and Peng Dehuai.

# BEFORE THE WAR

Following the collapse of the Qing Dynasty in 1911, China was consumed by a vacuum of power. Two major parties were formed, the Communist Party (CPC) and the Kuomintang Party.

EASTERN ROYAL TOMBS OF THE QING DYNASTY

SHANGHAI MASSACRE

# THE BEGINNING OF THE CIVIL WAR

The rivalry went on to become a war in 1927. Under the leadership of Kai-shek, the Kuomintang decided it was time to get rid of the Communist Party of China. The Kuomintang arrested and killed several of the CPC leaders in what became known as the Shanghai Massacre. As leader of the CPC, Zedong led an uprising against the Kuomintang, which uprising was named the Autumn Harvest Uprising. This uprising failed, however, this was the beginning of the civil war.

# TEN YEARS CIVIL WAR

The two sides fought from 1927 to 1936. Zedong led the common people and the peasants during uprisings against the Kuomintang while Kai-shek attempted to shut down these uprisings as well as eliminating Zedong and the CPC Army.

CHIANG KAI SHEK STATUE

CHINESE SOLDIERS

# WORLD WAR II

The Kuomintang and the CPC again united in 1937 when China was invaded by Japan to defend their homeland. The alliance continued throughout WWII, but both sides still mistrusted and hated one another.

# THE CIVIL WAR RENEWED

Both sides resumed their civil war in 1945, following the end of WWII. With the support of America, Kai-shek gained control over China's major cities. The CPC, however, had been greatly funded by the Soviet Union and was able to quickly gain support in rural areas.

WORLD WAR II

The CPC proceeded to launch an assault in Northern China, controlled by the Soviets. The Soviets assisted them by providing the weapons that were left by the Japanese. During the first few years of the war, the U.S. attempted to broker peace between these two sides by splitting the country. Neither side, however, was agreeable to this suggestion.

# THE END OF THE FIGHTING

The Communist Party of China was gaining momentum by 1948 and continued taking nationalist cities. With each of these victories, they gained support within China's population. The Communist Party of China captured Beijing in October of 1949. Declaring victory, they stated China was now under rule of the People's Republic of China. The nationalists proceeded to take off for Taiwan and established a government of their own known as the Republic of China.

STATUE OF MAO ZEDONG IN CHENGDU

Both governments today claim to be the legal government of China. In many ways, the Civil War has not ended, however, there has not been any fighting for several years.

MAUSOLEUM OF MAO ZEDONG

While he may have been controversial, Mao is remembered as a very important person in the history of the modern world, as well as a military strategist, a theorist, a visionary, and a poet.

For additional information about Mao Zedong you can visit your local library, research the internet, and ask questions of your teachers, family, and friends.

MAUSOLEUM OF MAO ZEDONG

Visit

BABY PROFESSOR
EDUCATION KIDS

www.BabyProfessorBooks.com
to download Free Baby Professor eBooks
and view our catalog of new and exciting
Children's Books